Wandering Minds
Meditation through coloring

DearingDraws
2015

"*To make no mistakes is not in the power of man; but from their errors and mistakes the wise and good learn wisdom for the future.*" - Plutarch

Content

Introduction

High school geometry was very challenging and complex during my younger years. Yet despite it's claims it did not explain reality as a whole. Neither did it teach me anything on a philosophical level. Well, those years have passed. And my views on geometry have changed quite a bit ever since I discovered Sacred Geometry, which is still geometry but in many ways cooler. I won't go into theory in this color book. For now I just want to say that these geometric forms have many levels of meaning. Sometimes even suggesting infinite levels of meaning. This can sound vague and transcendental. But that is because words don't have the capability to fully visualize the concept I am trying to communicate. And that is why I decided to tell stories of universal harmony through these designs. These geometric patterns try to take you to places where words cannot. It is about experiencing these mental forms and to freely create personal meaning into them yourself on a deeper level than language. Your role is to contemplate these visual stories and to bring those stories to life with colors. Make it your own story. Enjoy your journey.

And good luck!

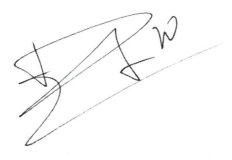

Coloring tips

These color pages are designed with a lot of thought and care. Some of the designs are quite detailed. So they can be quite challenging to color. That's why it can be helpful to have examples or suggestions of possible color schemes. If you want to see some examples of these pages can be colored please visit: *dearingdraws.com/wandering-minds-coloring-book*. I also post coloring suggestions on my social media channels:

- dearingdraws.com/wandering-minds-coloring-book/
- facebook.com/dearingdraws
- instagram.com/dearing_draws
- youtube.com/dearingwang

If you want to experiment with colors without wasting the book consider buying the E-Book. This is the digital version which can be downloaded and printed on A4 paper with you own printer. The benefit is that you can experiment with different colors and reprint all the designs as many times as you want. Enter the code '*38percent*' and get 38% discount on the purchase.

Let's get started!

"Happiness is not an ideal of reason, but of imagination." - Immanuel Kant

"Everything you can imagine is real." - Pablo Picasso

"A rock pile ceases to be a rock pile the moment a single man contemplates it, bearing within him the image of a cathedral." - Antoine de Saint-Exupery

"Imagination is the eye of the soul." - Joseph Joubert

"Imagination creates reality." - Richard Wagner

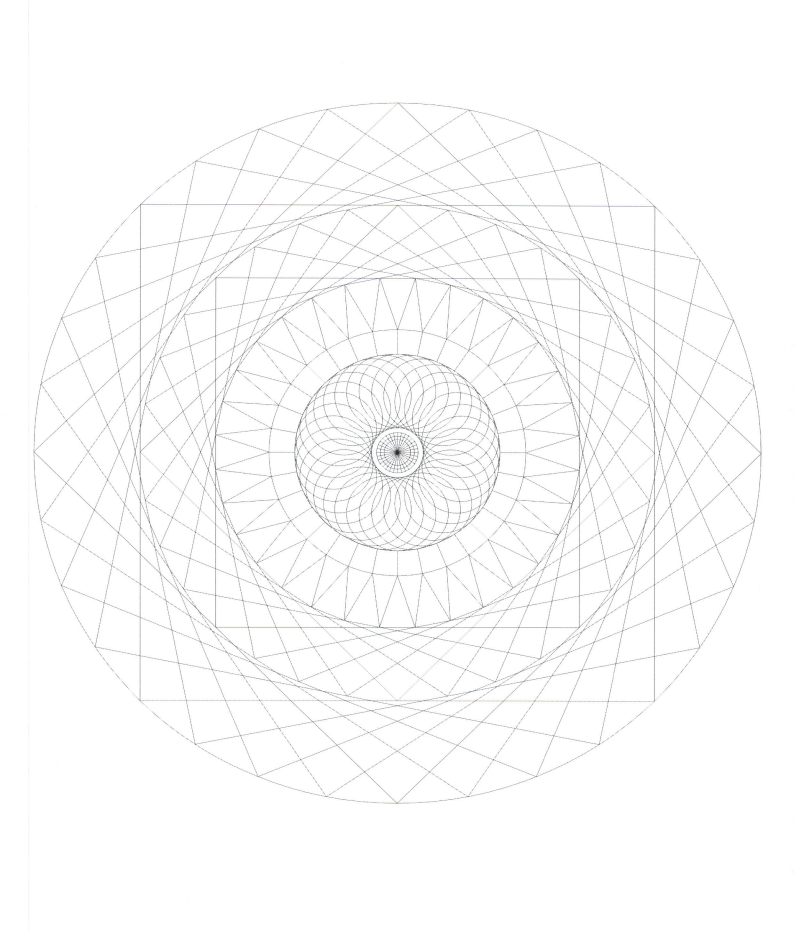

"Be content with what you have. Rejoice in the way things are. When you realize there is nothing lacking, the whole world belongs to you." - Lao Tzu

"Manifest plainness, embrace simplicity, reduce selfishness, have few desires." - Lao Tzu

"The wise man looks into space and he knows there is no limit." - Lao Tzu

"To know, is to know that you know nothing. That is the meaning of true knowledge." - Socrates

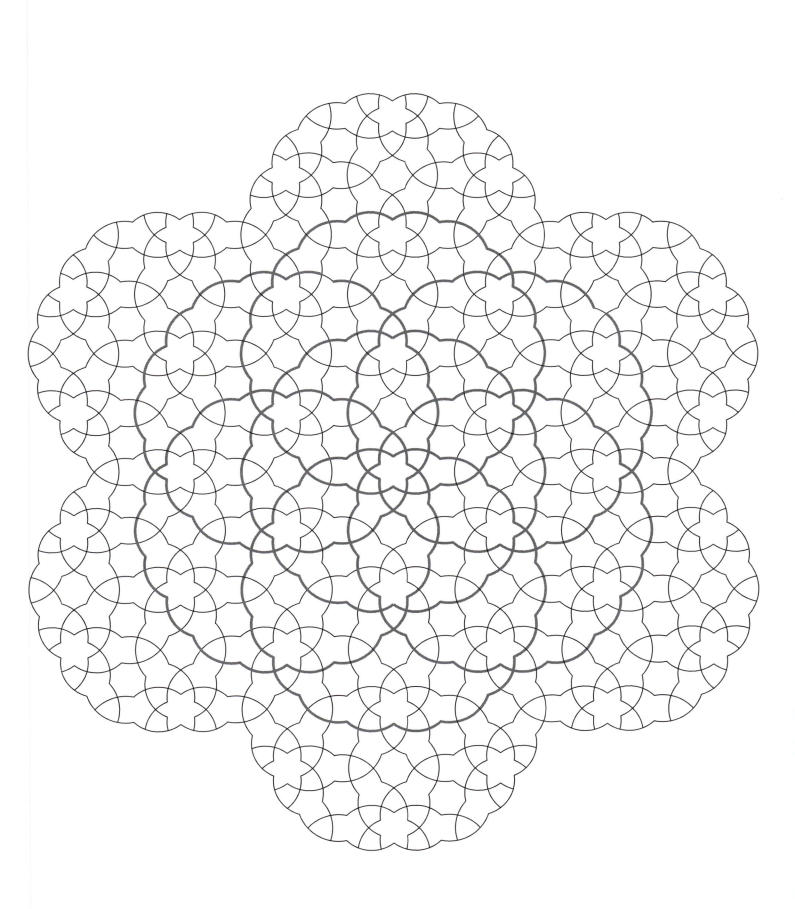

"Beauty in things exists in the mind which contemplates them." - David Hume

"The soul that sees beauty may sometimes walk alone." - Johann Wolfgang von Goethe

"The purpose of art is washing the dust of daily life off our souls." - Pablo Picasso

"The aim of art is not to represent the appearance of things, but their essence." - Aristotle

"The beginning is the most important part of the work." - Plato

"The pursuit, even of the best things, ought to be calm and tranquil." - Marcus Tullius Cicero

"A creative man is motivated by the desire to achieve, not by the desire to beat others."
- Ayn Rand

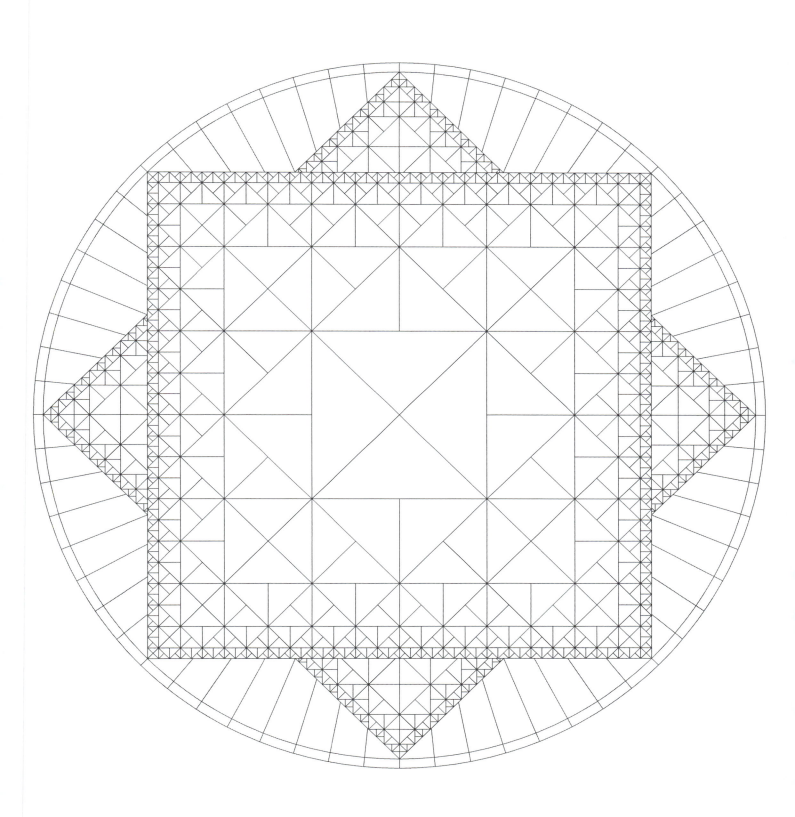

"It does not matter how slowly you go as long as you do not stop." - Confucius

"The secret of getting ahead is getting started." - Mark Twain

"There is only one corner of the universe you can be certain of improving, and that's your own self." - Aldous Huxley

"The only reason for time is so that everything doesn't happen at once." - Albert Einstein

"Life is not a problem to be solved, but a reality to be experienced." - Soren Kierkegaard

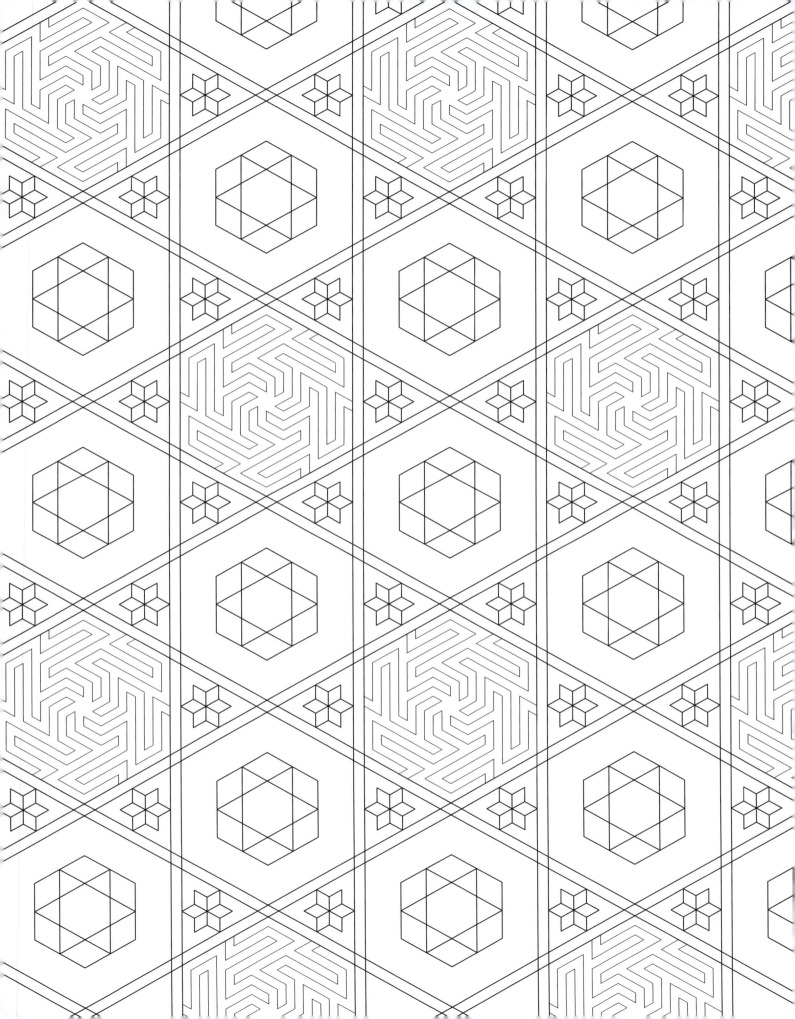

"Moonlight floods the whole sky from horizon to horizon. How much it can fill your room depends on its windows." - Rumi

"If you want to find the secrets of the universe, think in terms of energy, frequency and vibration." - Nikola Tesla

"The day science begins to study non-physical phenomena, it will make more progress in one decade than in all the previous centuries of its existence." - Nikola Tesla

"Most persons are so absorbed in the contemplation of the outside world that they are wholly oblivious to what is passing on within themselves." - Nikola Tesla

"Clay is molded to form a container. But being empty makes it useful. Doors and windows are cut to make a room, but it is the space that makes the room functional." - Lao Tzu

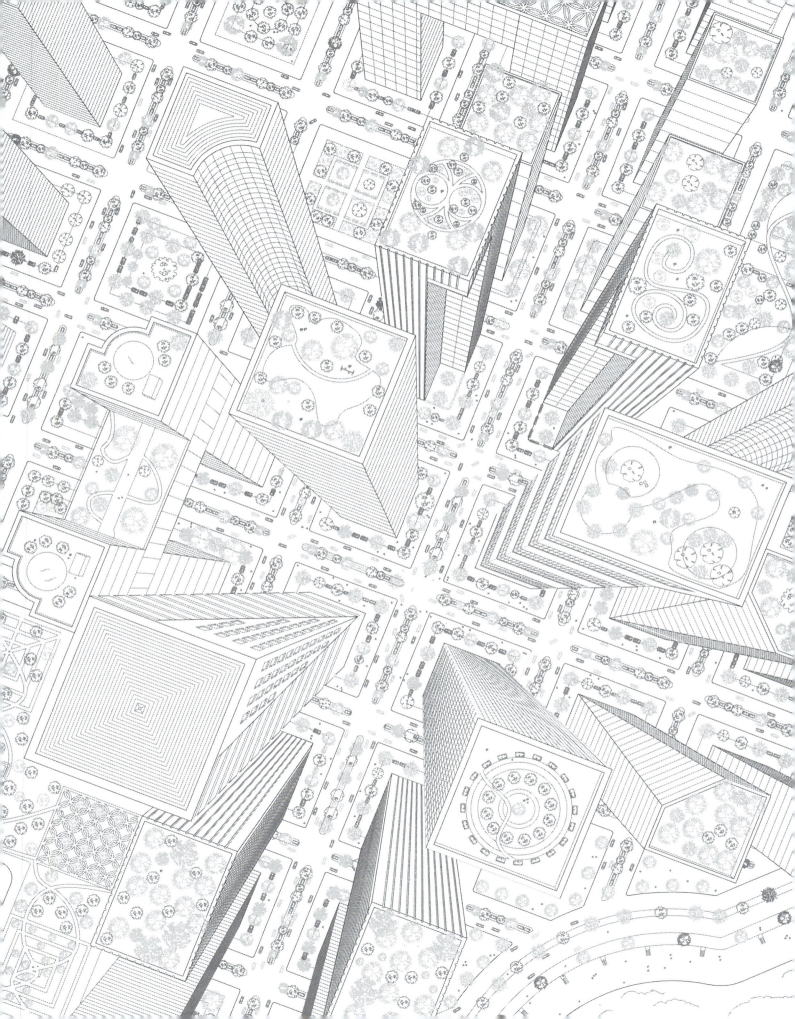

"I have just three things to teach: simplicity, patience, compassion. These 3 are your greatest treasures." - Lao Tzu

"Wisdom begins in wonder." - Socrates

"Be firm like a mountain, flow like a great river." - Lao Tzu

"Obstacles are those frightful things you see when you take your eyes off your goal."
- Henry Ford

"He who lives in harmony with himself lives in harmony with the universe."
- Marcus Aurelius

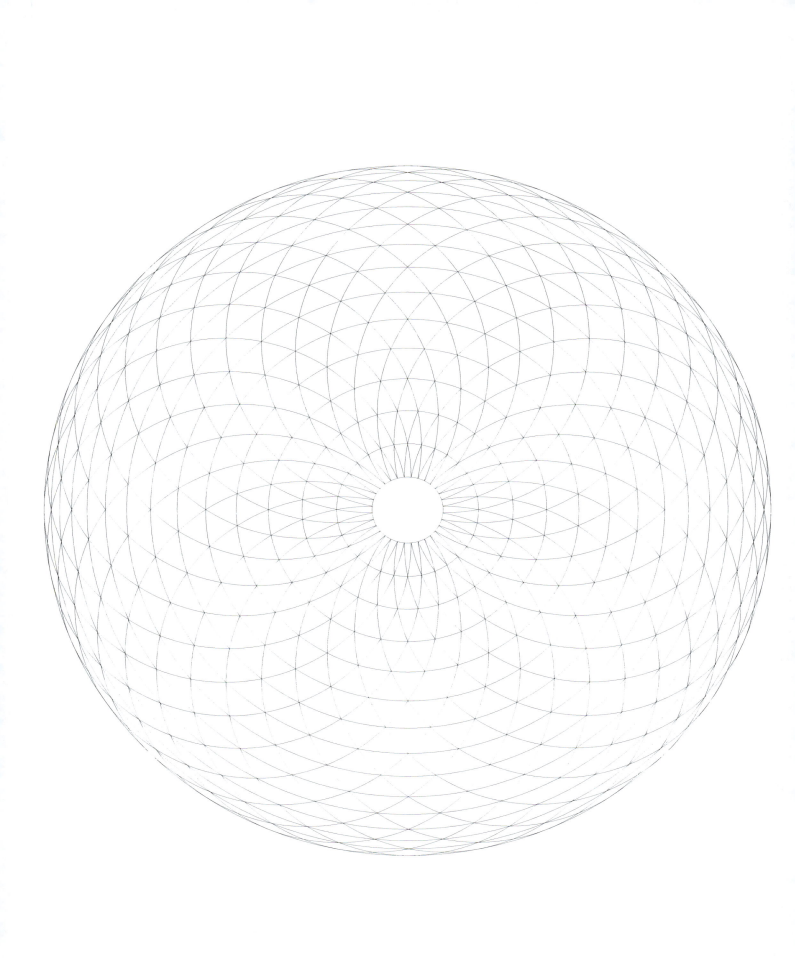

"Imagination is more important than knowledge." - Albert Einstein

"Happiness resides not in possessions, and not in gold. Happiness dwells in the soul"
- Democritus

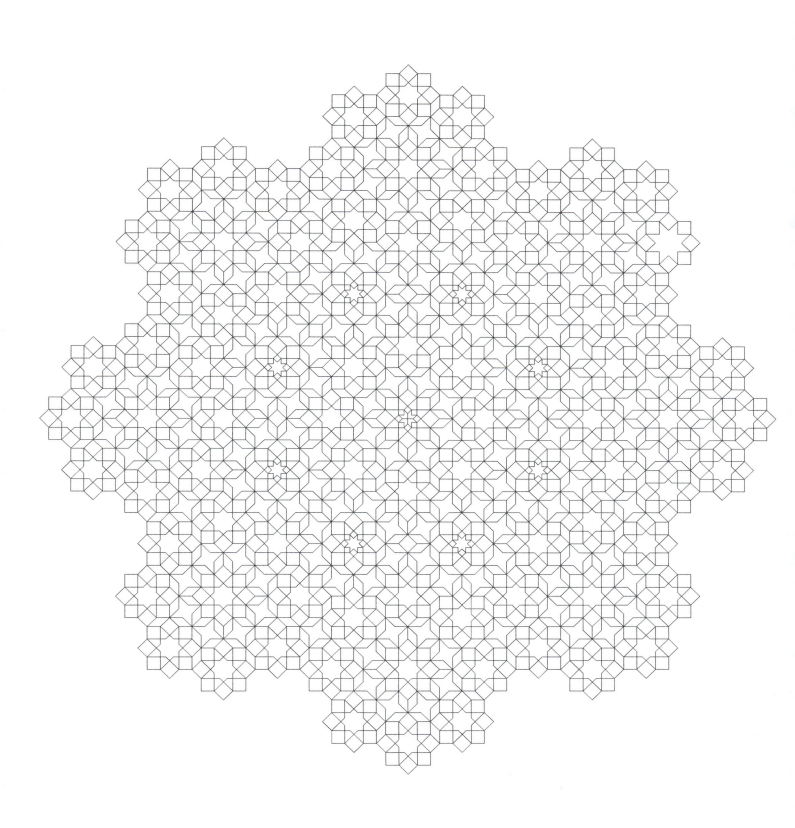

"I have noticed even people who claim everything is predestined, and that we can do nothing to change it, look before they cross the road." - Stephen Hawking

"Excellence is not a skill, it's an attitude." - Ralph Marston